american dust revisited

Also from Brian S. Ellis:

Uncontrolled Experiments In Freedom

Yesterday Won't Goodbye

American Dust Revisited

by Brian S. Ellis

Illustrations by Susannah Kelly

James!

I hope I keep surprizing you.

B. S. Ellis

This book published by University of Hell Press.
www.universityofhellpress.com

© 2013 Brian S. Ellis

Cover & Book Design by Vince Norris
www.norrisportfolio.com

Illustrations by Susannah Kelly
www.susannahkellyart.com

"Screaming" first appeared in *Radius*, August 2011.

"Imperfectionist America vs. the Downstairs Neighbors"
and "Napoleon-In-Rags Is Talking Shit about Your Band
in the Kitchen" first appeared in *Sparrow Ghost Anthology
Volume 2*, 2012.

Published in the United States of America.
ISBN 978-1-938753-06-0

Contents

Dedicated to:

Ken Arkind

Years ago
I was an angry young man
I'd pretend
That I was a billboard
Standing tall
By the side of the road
I fell in love
With a beautiful highway

– David Byrne, "(Nothing But) Flowers"

fire

Song of the Dog

Something went wrong the first time I first left the front
door of my first house and the time I never came back.
Something in the world made me disease and the orphan
that lived in my body took over. I learned to hate doors
because of everything that happened after them. They
called the orphan *interesting* but all I heard was *ugly*.
They used the word *special* but all I heard was *alone*. I
was rat nest hair unteachable in their sunshine problem.
I was every summer nine years old four a.m. watching
infomercials trying to scrub the love of death from my
eyes.

Nine years go by. My mouth is a carpeted bathroom.
Everything I have to say is stained.

Nine years go by. I spend my nights alley and curbside.
I make a living making sculptures out of other people's
discarded belongings. People tell me it's very artistic to
make beautiful things out of trash. I tell them that they
clearly don't know shit about recycling because there's no
such thing as trash. That was the only thing my mother
could tell me to keep me from crying about what my
teachers called me at school. My body is a dumpster I
sleep in. It's why I dream in fits about chain link fence.
Why my lust barks at abandoned Victorians. Why I
identify with paint rust. It's why we mouth the word dust
whenever we see photographs of ramshackle farms. I can
hear the words of twisted aluminum cans whispering
to me as I don't sleep. I know the begging of seam bare
sneakers and their prayers are why I never feel indoors.
All the traffic mangled bicycle wheels are banging down

my dreams. I hear the stories of those who have survived the worst and I cannot help but think of torn plastic bags emptying their soaking cardboard histories onto the highway. I cannot sleep in beds. My body is made of death and all of my words are rotten and I am thin enough to be your insides so I've come from the bottom of your mouth to tell you that you cannot make ugly things beautiful. We were never ugly to begin with. I am not broken because no one can tell me what my use is. Twenty-seven years ago I was not broken, Seventeen years ago I was not broken, Fifteen, Ten, Five, Zero, Zero, Zero is the number of people on planet earth who can tell me what my purpose is. Purpose is a song wailing out of every dirty noun trapped at the end of the night. This is the scream of the cornered. This is the song of the dog. Purpose is a song that does not end. Our origin lies somewhere in the future.

ll

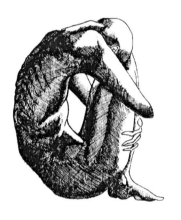

shame

Please, Wait

I was born with a body so frail
that weather passes through me.
As a child, hypothermia was a season.
My grandmother would pour cold water
over my shivering stubborn body.
It felt like fire.
As she rubbed my arms
and slapped my legs,
she told me that the burning was life
returning to my body.
That the pain I felt was the best possible answer.
That numbness was what to fear most.

There are billions of people in this world,
and there are billions of people inside of each of them.
There are millions of voices inside of me
who would see me dead.
I've heard all the arguments.

Sometimes it seems so inconsequential
that one life could not possibly matter.
Other times, we find ourselves
at the center of the maelstrom.
There are cameras in the walls.
There are cameras in my tears.

You can find the abyss anywhere.
You can tell those who have seen it—
we are never really indoors.
Our eyes are always out in the rain.

If you want it, the abyss will be there for you.
It is in no hurry,
so, do not hurry to it.
Yes, silence may be
the only perfect thing we can imagine.
Yes, death is beautiful
but it is not human.
It can never be more than it is;
it will not solve the argument of you.
I know that there is a nest of burn
and vomit in your skull.
That mirrors break your bones,
that your face is a knot of itch
gnashing against your sleep.
Your muscles are a collection of insults
and your teeth are frothing with blood.

I know that your hands are heavy
with these invisible rolls of quarters.
I know that your stomach is filled with dirty coins,
that you cannot pick up anything
or hold anyone, your fingers
wrapped around this thing you cannot see.

No one will ever be able to convince you
that life is worth living unless you let them
and then, it doesn't matter what they say
so I'll just beg you
wait.
Just wait.
You can always kill yourself tomorrow.
Please.

Heartbreak

The holiday always came unexpected—
the sudden Monday no-school of it.
How did this happen? No sleepover with Jeff Tanner,
no Sunday late night movies.
You find yourself alone in all of your twelve years
on a Monday morning no less. So,
you turn on the TV.
It's the Marathon.

Never mind the Sox.
This is Boston's main event.
The twenty-six point two two
(longer than New York!)
of our most twisted logic. The concave ear
of all of 495 turns to pay attention.

They say that running is mostly mental.
That, after the wall,
the real running begins. An act of
passion and freedom. Opening up the self
to move beyond the self.
Which is to say, an act of poetry.

As a pre-teen in the Blue Hills I learned
this is what a winner looks like:
collapsed on the finish line
skeletal, shaking, drenched in sweat,
weeping openly.

This is what I learned it means to be a Bostonian.
It doesn't matter if you win.

As long as you run.
As long as you stay stubborn
and vulnerable through all of it.

It's what you're going to be doing
for the rest of your life.
Running a crooked path,
exhausted and heartbroken.

Combination Locks
for my brothers

29. *Combination locks are built*
with a system of three rings.
The rings can spin independently
or co-currently, depending upon your movement.

Each ring has a notch on its edge,
analog to one of the numbers on the dial.
When the notch is moved into the correct position
the hammer slips, and the rings begin
to move together.

What the lock makers don't tell you
is that there are two sequences for every lock:
the right, that we all know,
and the unprinted left.

18. My father and I only speak at Thanksgiving.
We cannot speak to each other.
So we speak in facts:

In 1640 Richard Ellis emigrated from Wales.
He was a clock maker.
He was worried that the craftsmanship
of the woodworkers in the colonies was lacking.
So to make his grandfather clocks,
he hired coffin makers.
One such coffin still lives in my father's home.

27. After dinner, my father
shows me a small clock

he's been working on.
He tells me,
It had been running slow.
So I drilled tiny holes
in its pendulum. But now
it's running way too fast.
It's gaining time.

When he says this,
I wonder which one of us
he's talking about.

Engines No. 6

I am still wearing my garter belt
and fishnets under my jeans.
The needle on the gas gauge bounces
back and forth of its own accord.
Being empty and full all of the time.
Sarah is in the passenger seat.
I am hoping that when we get to her house,
she will invite me inside of it and ask
me to take off my garter belt.
Behind us is that shocking party.
Behind that is *Rocky Horror*.
I am behind the wheel
of my first love, a 1984 Oldsmobile station wagon.
We are forty-five minutes south of the city
when the car runs out of gas,
bucking forward in hard seizure,
in the middle lane of 495.

The two of us stumble on unlit interstate ditch
each in three-inch heels. I'm walking
to the nearest exit. *Do you know where
we're going?* Sarah wants to know.
I don't. She's wearing a little less
than a torn black tank top.
The Staties show up pretty quickly.
They don't like us: location, attitude, dress, etc.
How do you just run out of gas?
I don't have an answer.
*I've never been so glad to be in the back
of a police car!* Sarah tells them.

It is the first week of September
I am eighteen years old.
By the end of the month, my car will stop
working entirely, and I will park it
behind an ammunition shop
and take off the plates.

Sarah continues to not be wearing
anything that any reasonable person
would consider pants.
The one gallon of gas
gets the monster of my car
just barely to the nearest gas station.

Sarah is sixteen and hates her last name.
There is a lie we both want to believe.
The awareness of the costume,
which, at the time,
was the same as youth, was crushing.
I drive her home. I ask her to kiss me.
She says no, but another time.
I know it isn't true.

Lice

Years later, I can touch the back of my head
and still feel the wound.

The long trenches of open meat
eaten into the crest of bone.
The swarm of nightmare, gobbling flesh to fire,
the wound alive with the wriggling movement of the
insect.
The burning's habit of keeping you company.

The muscles will become too hot,
squirm on their own accord.
You will want to itch your surface off.
It will shame and rancid.
All the meanness of the back of my skull.
Sometimes, I find myself
talking through my blood mouth.

I wish my body was older than me.
That it always knew what to do.
I wish I didn't have to keep saving it.
I wish that I could be the younger sibling.

III

passion

Lift

Billie was sick and not getting better.
It was too simple, the common cold.
The inability to cope with it
undressed our poverty.

I lived inside of her life:
a shivering weight, broke, nightshouting
and jealous. Billie is not a woman
built for vulnerability.
It is an ill-fitting jacket.
But winter is constantly ready
to teach us new levels of humility.

Some nights she got so weak
she could not sit up in bed.
I would hold her, slip her arms
over my shoulders, and lift.
I am an un-strong man.
Except in this: I know what love is.

Love is not getting sick.
Love is practical. It has to be.
I had no other option.
Billie and I, we are not people of options.
Love is not an option.

The Things I Don't Have

Hunger does all the writing.
Hunger is the hardest worker.
Hunger is the only part of me clean-shaven.

At night, Hunger sits on my chest.
Stares into my open mouth,
paws my face like a cat.
Wakes me up from dreams about coffee
asks, *Why are we so poor?*

We are poor because we are defined
by what we don't have.
The poor paint their mirror-selves
in the ichor of nothing.

At night we wander hallways of kitchens.
Every door is a dead refrigerator filled with teeth.
Hunger is always willing to walk with me.
He asks, *Is the opposite of parents sex? Or children?*

The opposite of parents is strangers
who take our names.
People who use up the color
of the words that mean us.
Who make our names hollow.
The way that some make the word *love* hollow.

I make everything hollow.
Hunger tells me,
It is my magic. I make everything taste beautiful.
He gives me a handful of teeth,

I swallow them all at once
each incisor and molar bursting into sand as I chew.

I will always be your friend.
When all else leaves you.
Hunger smiles,
removing my right hand
and climbing back into my mouth.

How We Speak When We Do Not Have a Body

Her voice is all salt and open.
Every sentence is almost a question.
I say honest things, and it sounds alien,
because it is an act I commit at no other time.

I have wasted my entire life
pretending to be a coward.
I am slowly understanding
that pretense and actuality are one.

Here in the dark
with my first love,
I am very old.
Neither of us has to think
about our impossible life.
I love her voice
when I can hear the ocean in it.
She loves it when I say too much.
She loves me enough to hate me.

I cannot tell if we are touching.
I suppose we must be.
There is not enough room in the world
to do anything else.

Maps

Billie couldn't find her birth certificate.
She was standing in the middle of our room.
The summer was breathing all over us,
pressing its thumbs into our shoulders.
The duplex was not broken but slanted
warping with each steaming footstep.
I stood in the doorway, helpless.

And then the moment snapped—

The top drawer of the desk
all the inkless pens
dirty nubs of eraser
pins from comic book stores
the side drawers
blank and torn paper
folders of teenage prose
newspaper clippings
all of it, dumped onto the middle of the floor
the elephant statue, the Buddha
half a deck of playing cards
cut up National Geographics
old plane tickets
the blurry photographs of disposable cameras
handwritten letters from her to me.

When the entire room had been upturned,
the things each of us had chosen to keep
spread out across the room to see—
still, she did not find what she was looking for.
Her breathing slowed,

the rage returning to its natural weight.

Once again, Billie had punched
through the membrane of our relationship
to reveal it for what it was: a mess.
In all of its bitter honesty.
An honesty that I was slowly choosing
to despise her for.

Engines No. 2

Once, before I was a survivor
you could photograph everything about me.
Now everything I know
about my life is a fiction.
I was never brilliant candy sugar held to a strip
of paper. It didn't rain.
There was no puddle.
There was a terrifying man
waiting in the lightlessness
and it was me. I am the only monster.
I have always been the age I am right now.

When I Was Guilty

I drank sweat from rum bottles. I read books and didn't discern their meaning. When I wanted to be angry at someone I went to the ocean. It rained wherever I slept. I was arrogant enough to not have a home. I wrote poems about trains and thought that it meant something. I walked everywhere but had no movement.

I let the guilt become electric under my skin. I thought I was a snake charmer. I thought I could be mud if I was blind enough. I stared at the sun all day long. I used my taking advantage of someone to make people feel sorry for me. I bled pig tears. I kept going to the ocean. I collected twenty-three stones. I would not listen to what the ocean was telling me: the most dangerous part about wearing a coat of knives is other people seeing their reflection in the sheen.

IV

air

Allston Christmas

I made your bed unusable.
Forever impaired your trust muscle.
When the summer ended
you put me out with the rest of Allston's trash.

September is multitude. The year's face
is always younger.
For nine city blocks, dressers and paper lanterns
litter alleys like fallen chess pieces.
We lied about being gifts.
We are the breathing obsolete.
We are rapid with tarnish for the textured living of the
young.

I have forfeited the clarity of ritual
to brandish the bright flare of ugliness.
I begged for rain,
but had no roots to drink.
It rained anyway.

Kirk vs. the Squire of Gothos

Me and Piney move to the big city.
During the day we farm for graffiti.
At night we go fishing for boots.
At night, the night plays knife on me.
The cars have drums in them.
The river sleeps like a bow and arrow.
The voices are books in my bank account.
Eighteen pairs of golden hands took a piece of abandon.
I discovered why people ride bicycles:
it's important to have a high place to shout from.
It's why they grow radio towers from the hills.
I know a noise that listens.
I have a hard time listening to people who believe
microwaves exist.
There has barely been anything new.
I hear a sound coming;
it can be written exactly the way we write it:
the windows in the lungs,
the bodies made of wine.
There is a big sound filling our minds;
it follows us into the kitchen.
There is a sound coming.
I can see it with my mouth.

Driftwood

It's not that we didn't notice Piney building
a rowboat in the living room—
it's just that
he was unemployed, and had
this way of waking up under the morning.
I first noticed because of the smoke—
who doesn't want a cigarette while doing carpentry?
I told him, as long as he was crashing
he couldn't stink up the place any worse.

He painted it gray. The same color
as the ocean where we grew up,
the color of driftwood.
And soil too thin to bury anything.
It was christened with 22 ounces of Sierra Nevada.
The boat was named "Hank"
I asked Piney if that was his dad's name.
He said maybe.

Queen was going on and on, like he does
about the boat, that he couldn't get in or out of his room
because of the boat. So one night,
while Adam was cooking his laundry on the stove,
Piney announces he needs our help
getting Hank on the roof.
It got stuck in the bathroom hallway.

I was ready to give up—
but Adam was sure that if we
got the boat slippery enough,
we could squeeze it right through.

And I knew right away,
he was thinking of my pokeberry juice.
It took us a couple minutes to get it slick,
but once the three of us started pushing again
that rowboat popped outta that doorframe,
flying across the kitchen, out the back door
over the third floor porch,
and into the arms of an oak tree out back.

We never got it onto the roof,
just left it in the tree.
Piney went fishing every day.
Came home with a lot of cod,
sometimes haddock,
would barter fish at the package store for beer.

I never made my pokeberry wine
(although poisonous, I thought it would make a
powerful narcotic)
but even after Piney was gone
there was a rose memory-sweet streak
on the hallway wall.

A high watermark to point to.
The stain of Piney's empty days.
We could say, *Here, this.*

Ulysses S. Grant in the Time of Flowers

Ulysses S. Grant in the time of flowers
learned to boom boom like no one could.
Taught his hips the mandolin,
taught his hips the gamble of teeth,
bit through belts and door handles,
lifted handles of cucumbers to lips who knew it.
Spoke loudly of carnations and menthols
and swimming laps like a running grave,
how to live your life in the shadow
of your mother's tomb,
and the answer always came:
with your shirt off
at the tips of your fingers
licking summer's neck down
to the base of your girlfriend's
girlfriend's best friend's French horn.

Ulysses S. Grant in the time of flowers taught me
how to bicycle two times
so I could live Boston like a champion,
like our city could sneeze and make us that way.
We danced until every bedroom we knew was a disco
and discoed until the train woke
because the easiest way to remember
the night is to forget everything
that happened in those neon songs.
We forgot all those cocaine sunrises
and forgave the inner cowboy
because nobody gets skinny without help.

I met the sunshine on the other side of forever.

It was a textbook of sweat and sea charts.
It was something we could navigate to.
Our dance moves burned a glyph, a spell
to turn our voices into a flock of birds.
You flew across the ocean,
became our ambassador,
and any storyteller worth his salt will leave some details
in the sand.
So we will forget about your dealing with the Dutch.
We forget about the things you said
about Mary Todd Lincoln drunk on the Green Line.
We will forget about the buffalo body
hidden behind the breastplate.
We will forget the night.
We will forget the night.
And no one, no one,
will know what our sneakers looked like.
Because we were moving
too fast.

The Sound of Instruments Played in the Other Room, the Sound of Wind in the Kitchen

The VCR still has music in it—
there was a lifetime for the having,
between the fat tongue clunk of the end of the tape
and the high metal whir of rewind.
There was time enough to listen to your hand.
Time enough to be blue by and mean it.
The couch and the window and the shape
of the side of your face was a dream I had
been working on my whole life.
After all the years of time travel and invisibility
the taste of your voice was streetlight in my stomach.

Growing up, I had no idea I would ever be young
to trade careless in the glamour of bones,
or the light of teeth.
The razor torture of your skin did not write my name.
It didn't spell out yours either.
It just said *time* in thin, indestructible letters.
My whole life I had been working on a dream
where one day I was young, and I briefly
dated a beautiful woman who traded to me
all of her secrets for no other reason but her company
and we parted ways exactly when we needed to.
An ageless sphere, free of motive—

before the machines of ourselves clunked to a halt
and began spinning in the other direction.

Imperfectionist America vs. the Downstairs Neighbors

The Noise. Staggers through ceiling to take sleep.
To pinch itch.
My soaking plaster wags
a loveless bass in the face of work.
My bed cannot protect me. I have no night.
My apartment becomes a hackle, tensed.
They have the gall to write me notes:

Dear Neighbor,
We're sorry if the shows we've been having have been
keeping you up at night. We'd like to continue to have
them, but were wondering if there was a night of the week
that would be best for you, maybe we could move things
around. Either way, if we're bothering you give us a call,
or just come up.

I'm not giving these
art school dropouts the satisfaction.
I'm not bargaining with stupidity.
This neighborhood is bad enough.
With the street burping
its endless anonymous reggaeton
and the screaming pigs spilling out of the bars exactly at
one fifty-five each night.
I live in a soup of assholes.

Dear Downstairs Neighbor,
Let's find a way to work things out. We all want certain
things. We would like to make things as easy for you as
possible. Why don't you call one of us before the police?

There's no reason to be so isolated.

p.s. We're really sorry about St. Patrick's Day.

Don't they know where they live?
There are certain things you can and cannot do.
You need to be self-contained
when you live in buildings.
You have to protect yourself from the thinness of walls.
I refuse to let them bleed into me.
Can't they wait quietly for youth to die?
Can't they go to bars that will teach them sorrow?

Dear Ted,
We don't know why you refuse to talk to us. We don't
consider pounding on your ceiling proper communication.
We are not moving in the foreseeable future. We love
this neighborhood, its vitality and its vibrance. We are
trying to provide fun for our community. We are trying to
imagine the best possible world. Since you have not helped
us making things easier for you, we will continue to play
music whenever is convenient for us. Call the cops all
you want. It doesn't matter. We will pay any price. Don't
worry about the door handle you broke.

V

void

Charles

1.
All of my days begin by waking up and getting on the train. All of my days begin by waking up on the train and switching. All of my days begin by waking up and walking to work. All of my days begin by waking up on the ride home, switching trains, waking up again, walking home so I can go back to sleep so I can go to work. My days begin in the snap of body out of the land of dream so I can move from dream to dream underneath the earth. When I sleep on the train I dream about my life which involves waking up and falling asleep and dreaming. When I dream about dream in my sleep underneath the earth, I am underneath myself.

2.
I live off of Green Street. I change at Downtown Crossing. I work in Harvard Square. In between two cities are folded into patches of lightlessness. Above me a city is towering over my dreaming. Two maps are drawn to draw a third: first is the city that wakes, the second is the train that dreams, and I am the third. A map of colored thread. The cities and the river of the name of a man lost on the subway. Everything has sight and tells me about the looking. They tunnel inside of me. When I fall asleep, Green Street and Downtown Crossing are closer together. I am shrinking the city by living in it. I am an Orange thread. A Red thread. When I am a city, they are next to one another. I tunnel between the things that have tunneled into me.

3.
I pass the same street people every day.
No matter how many times I pass them
our interactions are the same.
My names for them are their questions for me.

Do you know the price of sleeping?
How do you feed hands?
Can you tell me the name of luck?

The names follow me into the tunnels
and I plant them under the city that I am.
The questions are at every stop.
The stops are all the same.
The locations and stops are questions
that I take into the dreaming. The faces
of buildings. The hands of sidewalks.

Do you know the price of luck?

The questions follow me home. They are
in my mouth when I wake up. I am asking
the watching sky, I am wading through
the river of my body.

How do you feed sleeping?

The voices are the same place
when I dream them together.
The city underneath the city alters
the space from meaning to meaning
from stop to stop, a third map is drawn.

Can you tell me the name of hands?

There is a necklace of questions
that lives its map in the city of my life.

4.
I can tell that I am awake because I am writing poems.
Poems are my work.
Poem is the place I leave home for.
I try to poem all of the nouns.
I am growing into them.
I am age at them.

Everything under and overneath the river and sky
all that touches the air and does not.
It is all dreaming into my mouth. I lessen the space
between them with the thread that I am.
Each thread a poem, an illuminated dream,
once they are inside of me
they wake up to their own dream
and then I am a city, a city that I poem.

5.
I can tell that I am asleep because I am writing poems.
When I move from train to train the dream changes.
When a dream changes meaning is made.
The dream is now a poem.
A poem is a dream all changed around.
My poems are my life:
a map of my city and my dreams at once.
One lives below the other.
They are connected by the subway.

6.
There are people making music
in the subway all the time.

They play guitar, the keyboard,
pots and pans, the music of my dreams.
They are everything this city is built over.
I am changed by the music, when this happens
the music is changed in me.
Poems are my music, changing my dreams.
The meaning maker is the sewing needle.
The music is the answer to all of my names.

7.
The train follows the train onto the train.
My sleep is underneath all that I have built.
It is a journey the city takes through me,
using the lightlessness of my dream,
to illuminate what I cannot see when awake.
The eyes of the nouns of the earth.
The music of the world.
A shimmering wall of sleep,
to hold us to
and connect us away from,
what is watching us.
I build a network of words
with a series of stops.

To try to map out my life STOP
I try to build a city STOP
I try to remember my dreams STOP
I dream my try remember STOP
The locations are wrong STOP
The words, a network STOP
I am trying to understand my dreams STOP
The dreams are a map STOP I am a dream STOP
I am a poem STOP I am Boston STOP When we STOP
I have to wake up STOP I have to keep STOP

moving STOP I STOP the wrong STOP location STOP
words the poem STOP
I can tell I am asleep because I am a poem STOP
I can tell I am Boston because I am a dream STOP
I can tell I am a poem because I wake up STOP

When the train stops I keep moving.
When I sleep I wake
to a city underneath my life.
When I wake up I collect
things for my dreams.

I dream to make poems.
I poem to make my waking.

The price of sleep is dreaming.
The price of dreaming is sight.
The price of sight is nouns.
The price of nouns is hands.
The price of hands is work.
My work is poems.
I am building a city of words.
I live in Boston.

**I Have a Few Announcements Before We Go Any
Further**

One: This is not a party. This is an experiment in
sustained exuberance. Of permanence in revel.
The concept is not to forsake tomorrow
in order to force imminence upon tonight,
but to let tomorrow and tonight
be what they already are;
the most important thing we've ever done.
And then, understand that forever.

Two: The carnival of returned dreams
has taken over your kitchen.
He's drinking all the unpasteurized milk in the fridge.
The carnival will repaint your house room by room,
until colors bloom from every corner, bright and eager,
they will seem to mock you on certain mornings,
mornings of carnivorous splinters and dehydration.
This is pretty standard. It's easy to hate ourselves.
We're big targets. Whatever I touch,
I have to use the outside of my body.

I was standing on the front porch
with Jackie Tangerine.
He was waving his arms in the air
and saying something
idiotic and perfect about beauty.
I didn't know what to say to him, poor kid,
I don't think that he knew that he was sunburnt.

I'm trying to be heard over the sound of my blood.
The goats in the courtyard

are erupting in fits of laughter
and the hens in the kitchen
have exquisite taste in modern culture.
They scratch and peck, but at least they spread seed.
They have come to shred your daydreams
and weave them into their roost.
This is your work at its finest.
The young and the super-young
have taken over your bed.
The velocity will not protect you.

This concludes the announcements.
Find your cups.

Talking Providence 1979
after Morgan Shaker

David Byrne and Edger Allen Poe go walking
uphill on Thayer Street in the autumn.
Poe's talking quickly, has his hand
around Byrne's elbow.
He pulls him all over the city.
Poe wants to meet some college girls,
buy some red wine, asks about scratch tickets.
Byrne is asking Poe about the patterns inside
the branches of the trees, if death is like
being made out of wood. Poe wants to do
somersaults on the lawn of Brown.
He wants to buy a gun. Figures they can cook a seagull.
Byrne asks Poe if he knows who invented shoes.
Byrne wants to know which parts of us are
the parasite, and which parts are the host.
They don't answer each other's questions.
They just keep asking faster.
They're talking over each other, laughing heartily,
slapping each other on the back.
They talk the history of wool, about mushrooms,
the machines in the sky, Byrne wants to go to the ocean
but at the mention of the Atlantic,
Poe becomes melancholy,
clutches his stomach like a holy man.
*There is a wave in the ocean
for each of my mistakes*, Poe says,
I am an album of unforgiven morals.
Byrne asks, *Is love a chemical, or a language?*
Poe says, *You don't find out when you die.*

Byrne says, *We're like the tin man and the scarecrow.*
Who the fuck are you talking about? Poe asks.
They're laughing again as they march
back to Benevolent.
Red wine easy in the smile,
yellow maple dry and noisy on salty cobble
and northeast crumbling brick.
Poe fades back into his haunt.
Pats Byrne on the shoulder,
until next time David, until next time.

Perishable

There is a population of every city
for whom the morning begins before the morning,
who live a series of yesterdays,
the people for whom the hours of the day
become muscles.

The New England Produce Market bares its mouth
to the toxin of the Atlantic, a concrete maw
perched on the pterodactyl wings of Boston.
Food is a door in the ocean.
It is a bridge from sweat to sweat.
Food marches dutifully on the backs of gold and oil
into miles of refrigerated bunkers,
into the cracked hands of yesterday's stewards.
Hands worn into gloves of themselves.

The guys call me Uruguay.
They asked where I was from
and I knew I could get a laugh.
The bosses don't like you to go into the storeroom.
They don't want you to see
the produce before you buy it.
Me with my two-wheeler amongst
the gas powered pallet jacks,
I'm at the bottom of the ladder.
But I make friends with the handlers
like Julio taught me.
They know me, call me Uruguay.
It's their job to give you the oldest eggplant.
You have to be fast to keep up with them,
to flip the eggplant over,

50

reveal the brown coins of time spent in the warehouse.
They're moving on, trying to pawn
a fifty-pound bag of wilted carrots,
and you're furiously dragging
the two-wheeler behind you
dodging the other vendors, trying not to lose an ankle.

The Produce Market protects its secrets
with bluster and muscles.
Muscles are time.
Time is bruises.
This is how we chisel ourselves into ourselves,
by what we march through.
Cold is not a feeling but where we live.
Where we work.
Cold is an inheritance.
The strength of our people.
It is how we slow the rot.
So we can gather warehouses
ripe with death.

Why the Unfreakable

Because reincarnation is class warfare.
Because reason is beyond Yes or No.
Because the places we have done will not die.
There is no thing to waste.

The junk grows breath
and sails through windows summer broken
takes out throats and begins to speak,
The Trash says, *Swallow all the sidewalks!*
Swallow the history of paper!
Swallow all the ink on all of the fingers,
then swallow the fingers!
I will drive discard-ance out of the soil
you built your cities on!

Because halfway across the earth disposable people
make disposable things so other disposable people
can throw them away.
Because this is what we burn fields of sand for.
Because this is the spine of oil.
Because this is what we're hollowing the earth out for.
Because this is what we're filling the earth up with.
Because at one point or another
we have all worn the name Trash.

The Trash says,
Napoleon masturbated nine times a day!
What makes you think you can be important?
There is a tally of all things made. Even as you learn
to speak satellite, you are writing novels
in pictograms of filth.

This entire city is my bedroom!
My mouth is an air conditioner!
I am your failure made flesh!

Because we cannot afford to make anyone disposable.
Because there is no straight line on planet earth.
Because each of us is slightly
bent into the curve of the globe
we just cannot see it.
Because there is a reckoning
growing in the lightless curve of the sphere.

Screaming

The problem with the sound of gunfire
is that it doesn't always sound like what it is.
Sometimes you hear a door breaking open,
sometimes you hear a guitar being unplugged
with the amp still on, sometimes
you hear your neighbor drop their end of the piano.
The problem is that sometimes
a prayer is not the first thing to escape your lips
but a curse, an annoyance
at what you thought was broken glass
when you could have been wishing time into reverse.
For another man's blood to return to his body.
Sometimes we are born
with other people's blood in our bodies.

The #39 bus had come to a screeching halt.
It was parked in the middle of Centre Street diagonal.
Open, empty, hazard lights on
frozen in time. The moment of someone else's decision.
The firefight must have been dazzling,
the gunshots spilling into the street,
flashing like dance lights
a narrative shocking enough
to demand a satisfying conclusion.
Twelve thirty-three in the morning
I was the only one on the sidewalk, I felt like a ghost.

Nothing is ever what it is.
It terrifies me to think
that no one reacts to car alarms.
The world is screaming at us

and we are so likely to sleep through it.
I would bargain my blood
to know where everything belonged.

Napoleon-In-Rags Is Talking Shit about Your Band in the Kitchen

There is something dead on the table.
Cluttered with the lost appendages of forgetfulness:
glass bottles, tin cans of liquor,
the shed accessories of nudity.
If there is a deficit between the ages
of you and everyone else in the kitchen,
you will grow older by that difference.
You were twenty-five when you pushed
through that door. By the time you perch
on that stool you're thirty-two.
And then there's this guy, in a beret.
He's leaning on the stove,
which is, in fact, your stove, but no one knows that yet.

On the other side of your life,
music is being strangled by the darkness
your ankles are drowning in weekdays
and you spend most nights
trying not to look your bedroom in the eye.
You finally found everything your adolescence
was missing and it tastes infantile.
And then there's this guy,
in a beret
he's really leaning on the stove. He's got the room.
He's holding court. He's got time to suck his teeth.
His facetious knowledge of the zeitgeist
makes your mind feel like a sieve.
You want to argue the mechanics
of his deconstruction of the newer generations
but the only thing you're an authority on

is recipes for your own sadness.

With your self-pity polished to its sharpest:
the eleven thirty-five of the universe—let's call it.
You want someone to give you credit
for the years you spent as ghost.
The torture of trading your wisdom
for the secret of invisibility
is that you can't show it to anyone.
Even if you were going to corner Saturday Night
in the piano room the way you've always dreamed,
what are you going to do?
Point at the nothingness that is your chest
with a finger that is not there and say,
See? See?

Alice Wrinkle

Alice Wrinkle moved her hair all around
in that way that made me crazy.
It didn't help that we only
ever saw each other in other people's bedrooms.
It didn't help that she called me a different name
every time she saw me.
She looked so good sitting on wooden floors.
I wanted to call everyone who ever called me
a sewer rat in high school.
Wanted to borrow Alice's phone and hold
the speaker up to the inside of the third floor windows
just so all the teenage public bathroom mirrors
would answer.
I would explain this
to Alice and she would smile
and I knew I was banana split cream pie trouble.

All the cephalopods were in love with her.
She sounded like a bus leaving after it's gone.
She had stories from every city I wanted to go to
and a sister in Nicaragua.
Her VHS eyes made me forget
about our class difference.
I talked about books she never read,
I pretended to have seen the films she loved.
Science magazines wrote her letters.

Alice Wrinkle could let the magic out
of every breathy antique pendant
until our walks were grandmother soft
until I was no longer ashamed of my knuckles

or my mouth.
This is the winter cast in brass.
Wasn't it warmer than you remember?
Here's the autumn in corduroy,
not as hard on the eyes
and as long as we're going backwards in time
let's summer our hair together.

Your neck is a horse.
It feels like we're swimming all the time.

I saw Alice Wrinkle not that long ago
right around my birthday on the wrong coast
after I had stopped being young the second time
but before the third began.
She had her arm around the waist
of some boring or dead guy,
I know that zombies were kind of a fad that year.
When she saw me, she waved excitedly
and called me Stephen.
I wondered if she knew something I didn't.

There Is a Reason We Do Not Lock the Front Door

Love is a word that is simple in the moment
but becomes dangerous over time.
Promise unfulfilled is a sharp thing
that lives in the body, makes some places
difficult to touch.

So this is the time in the history of the world
that we lived together. Somewhere between the sound
and the games, the spirits and the voices,
while we were waiting for something important to
happen, something important happened.
While I was watching the sky
for the great golden wave,
your heart became a part of my shoulder.

Intimacy runs on its own clock
most of the time it arrives slow
but always unannounced.
I think that it happened while I was pacing the
bathroom hallway
that is the ages between twenty-three and twenty-seven.
Sometime between our attempt to resurrect the Polaroid
and our attempt to resurrect the cassette tape.

While we were both standing awkwardly
in the upstairs bathroom;
you, having just been left by whatshizname, and me,
makeup smeared all over my face,
wearing only those gold lamé tights
I would later leave in Denver,
you asked me, *Is a moment really a moment*

if you can't leave it?

There is a reason we do not lock the front door.
It's not just a matter of trying to prove
that we were once what we say we are now.
All the low light kitchen table prophesies
made in the witness of stillness.
All the late night half songs and empires of friendship.
It wasn't just one stop on some larger train.
Wasn't an experiment in ego and sex.

The path out, by necessity, paves a path back in.
The rust is still framed in the parlor,
the noise is still lighting the basement,
sing-a-longs grow in the carpet,
and just when you think you're too tired to sing
someone else's song,
the vibration takes your wrists in its hunt.

You're gone.
And I'm still here.
Between us is a shimmering veneer of choices.

There is no battle to be done with the ghosts
of who we already are in the future.
Sometime, the building where we left our memories will
be gone.
Leveled for some other kind of city
but nothing will have been erased.
It doesn't mean that we didn't write
our own hobbled utopia
into a million strangers' timelines.

The house is still here,

and when I say house, what I mean is
I'm still breathing.
No matter how far you move from it,
Home is exactly that.

VI

gold

Engines No. 5

The engine is off.
It is an unnatural state for a bus.
Seems the bus ought to be born rumbling, throat aroar.
I had been dreaming about being awake
and the movement. The cold glow
of the colorless mountains
that are a rusty bruise in the sun
now takes up the drained fluorescence of a dead planet.
Around me are the growls
and milky nose whistles of sleep.
It's just me and the driver awake.
I can see his face, in the reflection of the rear-view,
he has a reading light on, sighs powerfully.
I become afraid.
The bus isn't moving.
It's on the side of the highway.
Without breath the machine is dangerous.
This is no shelter.
It's the opposite.
As if he senses my fear the driver looks at me.
There is a light rising from behind the mountains.
It could be the sun.
Or a city on fire.

Denise Asked

There was a sign of instructions
next to the front door.
No cameras, one at a time, etc.
It was hand painted.
Inside the apartment was dark
and divided into a series
of chambers with red velvet curtains. Soft jazz played.
The part of me that can sense humans
knew there were people behind
the velvet even though nothing in particular
could be heard. Breathing. Heat.

She was fifteen years older than I am.
Had long dark hair, and wore a white slip.
I wanted to be polite, to make her happy.
She led me to a back room.
There was a fake potted plant, thick brown
carpet and a deep-seated leather chair.
There were two small tables on either side
of the chair. The tables and the wide arms of the chair
had small white towels folded on them.
She told me it was a hundred dollars plus tip.
I asked her how much tip usually was
That depends, she said.
I didn't have any cash,
she takes credit card. I took out my wallet
and handed a card to her: two hundred.
She left the room and closed the door.

Earlier that day, Denise had asked me,
Would you pay for sex?

I said, *No.*
Then amended, *I hope not.*

It was taking way too long with my card
but I was sure if I opened that door
a large man was going to leap out of the shadows
and bop me on the head.
I opened the door anyway.
I saw bright fluorescent light glaring behind red velvet.
She was sitting on the vinyl floor of a small kitchen
hopelessly jamming buttons on a credit card machine.
The cashier in me took over.
I sat down and took the reader in my hands.
I tried everything: on/off, different settings,
clear, enter, reset.

The slip she was wearing was not made
for sitting cross-legged on the floor.
No underwear, entire left breast,
she was twenty years older now.

There was a dry erase board
on the wall with a schedule.
Prostitutes have time cards, marketing departments,
assistant managers. We all lead regular lives.
Sitting on a cold floor under the blemish sharp light,
we both started laughing.
She told me that if I went to the bank machine
it would be really inexpensive.
The way she said *bank machine*
it sounded like a delicate night flower.
She kissed me on the cheek,
and I was free to go be the person
that I tell people that I am.

Engines No. 3

I am still awake in the Greyhound station in Phoenix.
My phone is dead and anyway there's no one to call.
I shuffle from one Formica table to another,
drunk on weakness, sliding
my tiredness under the chair.
Six hours deep, Tina asks if I have a book to read.
I didn't know her name when she asked.
She is wearing sweatpants that have the word *Slut*
printed on them, in quotes.
I have similar pants.
We exchanged names and destinations.
Her teeth are made of rhinestones.
My teeth are made of coffee.
She has the kind of face that I think that I recognize
because I think I have the same kind of face and
it is the face of a person who has had the shit beat
out of them for having a body.
Tina's bus to L.A. was full.
She's waiting in hot pink patience
in the early morning grime.
I hand her a novel that I liked.
We read together for a while,
I consider asking Tina if she has a razor to cut
my eyes off my face but instead I fall asleep sitting up.

Semi-Professional Dog Racing in Central California

His name was Gunner, or Harmon.
I couldn't tell, the way he talked
outta the side of his face.
The first thing he told me was,
Don't try and smoke in Sacramento.

Michelle has never been on a bus before.
She can't believe we didn't get patted down.

Six-Five stands the whole trip
says his legs can't take it.

It's a precise kind of person
who takes thirty-hour bus rides.
The bad kids pick each other out at the first smoke stop,
pass brown bags between seats.

Michelle is convinced there's a bomb on the bus
anyone could have snuck it on.
Her ringtone is Shaggy's "It Wasn't Me."
But it always stops right after
she caught me on the counter.

Six-Five keeps asking for a light.
I keep telling him I don't have one.

We get to Sacramento
and what is the first thing
Gunner or Harmon does?
He asks me if I want to go smoke.
So we do, and while rolling one on a side street

behind the bus station, a cruiser pulls up.
For some reason, Harmon bolts.
The sirens wake up and lift off.
The rest of us have to get back on the bus.

Six-Five asks me for a light.
I'm beginning to wonder if I understand the question.

We're in L.A. before I realize about Harmon's bags.
They had last seen sky in Portland, Oregon,
slept like fitful birds in a wandering room
and ended somewhere unimaginable.
The bags had followed a tunnel,
emptied into a brilliant divorce,
found themselves older
than the world had ever intended.

Engines No. 8

We took the ferry across the sound.
The ferry began on the West Coast
and the island was even farther out.
When we reached the island we got
back in the pickup.
In the pickup we kept going,
past the quaint island village past the salty farms.
The edge of the world wasn't even visible behind us.
My ghost is pushing against the salt.
I am screaming in the bathroom.
I am alone in the hotel bar.
Death growls in the lungs
but it is not enough to die.
I want more than death.
We curled dirt back roads to see
where the road ended because we didn't
think that it did but then it did.

There was a circular gravel lot
and some evergreen and past the trees
the ocean that I cannot help but think
is clean and perfect but I know it's not,
like a dream. There was a garden of totems.
Denise and I walked amongst them,
and they reminded me of the ocean except
with fewer voices. Denise and I shared a feeling
that we didn't have to talk about.
It was the feeling of feeling good and small,
and that somewhere there are still adults
in the world even though most adults you meet
turn out to be children.

It was a feeling so different from
the furious-blood-and-thunderstorms-
of-guilt-in-the-theatre-of-nightmares.
We let Denise's huge dog out of the pickup
and he knew what to do.
He made love to the sky with his entire face.
He ran and ran and felt everything.

Engines No. 7

I can hear the yelling before
I knew where it came from.
Two suitcases wrenching
my arms from my shoulders,
I stumble through the closed fast food
drive-thru. There were two men sitting
on the steps of the bus station and one
woman, moving quickly all around the lot.

She was kind of dancing,
swooping in mighty decisions.
She was wearing a trash bag.
One of the men was small, worn like leather
and clearly being eaten alive from the inside.
The other man was massive, swollen in every direction,
pus thick. Big-Man was yelling at the woman.
He said the worst things I've ever heard.
There was a normality to it that frightened me.
This was not a climatic moment in anyone's life.
Big-Man's long greasy gray hair
swung around like a fire hose.
She was beyond him. Whatever violence raged
inside of her kept her deaf to everything else.

It was four twenty-three in the morning.
The bus station was alive and festering.
Two TVs blared the news
a man in a baseball cap and no shirt
humped an arcade game
a teenage girl leaned against the wall
next to a payphone that rang incessantly.

The police arrived outside.
They talked to the woman in the trash bag.
She screamed as powerfully as she could.
She unloaded the history of her life
into a single proud tone:
a sound to pierce the nature of unfairness.
They took her away.
There are monsters worse than crack cocaine.

Big-Man came inside the station
and marched to the bathroom.
He vomited so loudly the entire
bus station could hear it.
So loudly we could visualize the blood
torn from his throat.

I don't know where I'm going.
I think I am from here.
The blood in the toilet is the blood inside of me.

VII

blood

On Top of Book Mountain

The train makes a sound that undoes sound.
The shhh of retreat,
matches unlighting themselves,
snow wanders in its sleep.
A mile out of my window,
I see campfires dotting the wooly dark.
They draw close and pull back,
crisscrossing the nowhere
in every direction.
They are not campfires.
They are highway cars
wands of silence.
There is no dark either.
Just land without light
there are no stars.
And no time.
I worry about the air shattering from its thinness,
the world's weight.
We are close to the top.
Between the hours and the divide.

Engines No. 4

Travel is a constant dollhouse.
Every day I fold sheets and blankets
in a tiny version of my life.
I stay for a week in Denver
living in someone else's apartment.
Different favorite coffee shop, different girlfriend,
different bar. I can tell I am not me
because I have no tolerance here.
The nights I spent practicing drinking are gone.
They are living a life of their own at sea level.
Across three time zones tokens of a new life
have taken up nests in my pockets.
My suitcases are threadbare
and from the early eighties, like me.
Their seams bulge under the weight
of strangers writing themselves into my life.
Everywhere I go the hands of the helpful
are offering gifts for the filling. *Thank you,*
yes, I can't listen to this CD on the train
but I will be sure to when I get home!
If I were good at carrying things I would have
stayed in one place. So I edit.
I leave ingredients in borrowed homes.
Chicago gets Pittsburgh's cassettes
hidden in the bathroom mirror.
Cleveland's poems are slipped
into a bookshelf in Omaha.
I leave an entire library in Denver.
I hold nothing.
I am anti body.
Denver is the hometown of snow.

You can watch it materialize, fat and innocent.
Even lying drunk in the middle of street,
you're still a mile up.
You're in the air.
You're flying.

There Were Rivers Here

The train sees the rusted part of every town.
In the desert, there's no reason to bury anything.
The skeletons bleach reckless.
Trees are sculptures of melting.
Sage congeals in ditches, looks like sea moss.
Husks of farm machines wilt in dry air
bent into smokes' twisty-ness.

These mountains made of faces terrify me.
I only understand the bloodstream.
I am of the ocean's family.
I will never forgive myself for having bones.

Nevada

Who left all these rusted halves
of pickup trucks, alone, here in the desert?

Pig Pen

This nice guy from Indiana,
he can't keep his limbs in one place,
his glasses won't stay on his face,
the straps on his overalls keep slipping,
his hair is loose in a ponytail;
but not for long. He's playing cards
with the two squarehead bros from Michigan.
I'm sitting with the older guy. He's from Utah
but just came from New Orleans.
We're in the lounge car. The train is cutting
through Colorado, one mountain pass at a time.

The lounge car attendant is locking up. It's after one.
Indiana asks if he can play his guitar.
As long as it's not too loud.

When the attendant is gone,
the older guy takes the bottle of whiskey
out from under his seat. He tells me
he's been riding the train since he got divorced.
Kids are grown and won't talk to him.
Indiana is launching into some Grateful Dead
but he only knows Pig Pen tunes.

The older guy tells me that he had always
wanted to do this. That he wanted to do it
when he was my age. I get this look often,
that I am not a person but a shadow of an other.
A relic of opportunity.

The bottle gets passed around.

The group of us struggle through
a version of "The Weight."
Indiana and I go to the bathroom
and swallow an eighth of mushrooms each.
When we get back
the older guy is alone.

I stay drinking with him.
The train lights have been turned to sleep.
The older guy tells me he had been
volunteering for the McCain campaign.
He shrugs. He knows it's not as popular
with the younger crowd. His voice
came down with the lights.

He asks me if I read the Bible
but then says it doesn't matter.
He asks me if I know about the Antichrist.
How the end will come as a promise
of a golden age.
How the Antichrist will have a silver tongue.
He tells me that he's never listened
to a Barack Obama speech, and never will.
He tells me he's scared.
I'm scared too.
I don't know how we got here.
The train sleeps and keeps moving.

Engines No. 9

To be woken by a stranger from
a dream is to experience
the shock of seeing a face that
you have never made. If your
stop is in the middle of the night,
the conductor will wake you.
The train is gloom and motionlessness.
The conductor's voice is a handful of fog.
Move this curtain curtain.

It is snowing in Nebraska. Winter
lives in a steep grade. I can feel
the air twist in the air. There are
invisible rivers, the invisible
that lives in the invisible.
The fuel that lives in the fuel.
The train depot is closed and it is
too late for color. Lincoln
is an old photograph of itself.
I set my briefcases down and they
make no sound. When I set my briefcases
down the train vanishes. When the train
leaves it was never here.

I don't remember when I became
a salesman. Now my voice has sold
me to the movement. Now my voice
has sold me to the central time zone.
Now is the danger of inventing.
The engine in the engine.
Now never moves.

All I have is a telephone number.
The payphone works so I must be
in the past. If this doesn't work
I'll have to disappear. There is
no backup plan. The earth
is rolling under my imagining.
The telephone rings.
The telephone rings.

VIII

ghost

The Eisenhower Interstate System

And then Wyoming becomes not only
the place I'm driving but an emotion.
I close my eyes.
Greg and Sam are fetal'd into gurgling half sleep.
I drive for twenty-two, twenty-three miles
with my eyes closed.
The earth is an ultraviolet drumhead screaming
to silence pitch above the air in every direction.
My body, the hungry balloon
sand bright in gasoline script.
I can see the dinosaur of Nevada
slowly wading through the glaciers
lost under the false compass of Venus.
I can see the earth above and below me
doppelganger clouds dive under the ocean of scraping.
I can see:
The ghosts of horses trapped inside of speed.
The hearts of pure machine.
The land of no house.
The highway: sky.

I watch my body move beyond my body.
I am crying, but I know that tears
will bring me back to the ground.
I have been starving to be outside of myself.
I cannot breathe out
or I will lose the flight.
I will lose the life impossible.

The Eisenhower Interstate System
was declared complete

on September 15th, 1991
when the last stoplight was taken out of I-90
in Wallace, Idaho.
You can go for days without ever opening your eyes.
Some people go their whole lives.

The Last Payphone

The payphone at Yellowstone
has a two-hinged glass door.
I am shivering from the rain and the hour
I drop my sticky car floor quarters
and the torn journal paper
with your number that took me three tries to get,
turning my dead cell phone on again and again
getting a couple of digits each time.
Paper between my teeth I need two hands
to get the coins in the slot,
sometimes my hands don't work so well.
The glass fogs from breathing and body heat
and the ocean green hive light blurs
over the closed ranger station.
First time I do the dialing and coins in the wrong order.
The fist of sound of the quarters coming back to me
rings in my chest.
I will feed as long as I can stand.
I get it right the second time. I heard your phone ring,
the complete regular sound of it,
all day I had been backseat of the Sentra
with alkaline worries boiling
not being able to talk to you.
You're not picking up on purpose, I know it.
After three tries I hang up,
because I can't waste quarters.

I put the flat of my hand on the door.
I felt as heavy as all of the animals.
I breathed a little bit.

I put the quarters back into the machine.
It rings again but this time I hate it.
Each ring cuts my hair. It is a bad shave.
When your voicemail wakes up to mock me,
I tell it everything. Every detail I have in my brain.
I babble and curse
and swear and promise.
This is the last payphone on earth
and I am making my stand.
I will always hate you for this. How many times in my
life had my voice saved me?
And wasn't I practiced at it already?
I didn't want to come here.
I never wanted my love to be poetry.
But now it's all over the floor.
Now it lives amongst the trees.
We will never be what we were.

The Badlands

The landscape of The Badlands
is made from the bones of chalk.
As you climb her teeth,
even the smallest of incisors,
guilt comes off in your hands,
ballooning into unending wind.

I know there are bison on the moon.
This much is certain—

Dust is an angry sibling.

The wind knows I am a kite.
Her daughters circle my tent at night
pound their delirious song of no rhythm into me.

Me and my friends met a ghost named Joe Barre.
You'd be surprised to learn how many ghosts
live in RVs. I knew he was a ghost
because he kept repeating his name so often.
Sometimes, even our dream-selves are bald.

Ghosts always want to talk about death.
They're extremely forgetful.
The wind keeps taking what they know.
The way the wind
keeps promising
to peel away my feet,
my legs, my body,
wash skin to flint.

Engines No. 1

Matt's band is called Viking Fuck.
He doesn't live at the house anymore
but he's the one who organized the show.
Adam and I get there early
and the place is empty except video games.
To my surprise it fills up quick
partly because it's Iowa
partly because it's raining
partly because the Townies
have a deep need to out-party the students.

The gang discovers I'm over twenty-one
so a last minute beer mission is formed.
Matt and I run to the only open store.
Matt's long baseball player's legs
charge through slick heartland grid.
We slow down as we go.
Our troop gaining number as we move.

Outside the convenience store
is Cynthia, a sixty-something-
year-old transsexual veteran.
She's got cash but has been kicked
out of every alcohol selling establishment in the county.
We bring her back to the party.

She was discharged from the Navy
in the late sixties. Got deep into psychedelics.
When the omni-chromatic fog cleared
it was the early eighties and she was the lead singer
in a vaguely popular Genesis cover band.

Phil, she tells me (she speaks his name intimately),
was sent from a higher plane
to emancipate the human mind.

She has an endless supply of weed.
She packs bowl after bowl as the
outrageous energy of young America
rages around us. She offers
her life's myth over the fire.

This is why we drive.
Why we west.
These are the nights
the devil-headed gambling bears
its own feverish apples.
Cynthia keeps repeating
I have a bit of Morrison in me
and touches my chest unnecessarily.

Viking Fuck wails in the basement.
Cynthia offers me an assortment
of pills out of her grab bag.
The bowl sat smoking on the table.
A shirtless teenage boy came
and snatched it up, when he did
a bit of smoke spit
out of the glass piece's mouth
it hovered: a tiny storm
gathering over the table.

Return of the A.M.

Adam and I and the Jeep full of trash
between Kansas City and Lincoln.
We had made one stop all day:
to jump in a Little River named Little River.

All the windows are down and Adam
has his underwear out the window, and it was
working way better than I thought it would.

We were behind
because we had spent the entire day before
looking for the birthplace of Captain Kirk,
so I was becoming familiar
with the deep end of the accelerator
and the air babbled every inch of us and
the radio was on but it just played static
and we listened to the static, it was the sound
of all that open country.
The sound of the magnets in the soil,
the ones that pull people
and entire families into the earth.
The sound of an earth that never stops touching the sky.
Here's me and my friend Adam,
awash in the white noise
of the abandoned heartland.

The curtain of static parted
and a man's voice came on the radio:
kettle-warm, slow, just.
His voice transformed all of the contents of the Jeep,
one by one, until loneliness was scattered as far as the

sunshine could reach.

All of the trash we carried became tools, instruments.
Now we had a banjo, a tent, pots and pans,
drums, a gas stove, and a typewriter.
Instead of being the things we could not divorce,
these were the parts of our memories
to make more memories.

Let the empire fall
shake all the neon out of space,
even if we are deserted by
all the banker-kings tomorrow,
there will still be this:

Lone voices. Living on the edge of nowhere,
stranded in the middle of freedom.
Folks who spend their days spooling copper wire
to write love songs into the wind.

He put on an old big band tune.
You could hear the crackle in our shared history.
When it was over, he thanked God
and I didn't get mad at him for it.
He never said his name.

The God of Gift Certificates

The god of gift certificates
lives in Lincoln, Nebraska.
She walks the edges of strip mall
parking lots at dawn, taking slow even
RV-long strides. Her legs
a warped railroad coin copper.
Her bare feet torn and blushed
as the naked Midwestern sunrise.
She stands sixteen heads tall to the shoulder.
Her eyes are the points of light
rubies dare to grow into,
set in a fog of darkness.
Her hands, each a holiday.
Her voiceless lips a golden cursive.
Her simple dress, cigarette finger yellow.
The hem is loose, ragged,
a strip of torn cloth so long
the poem of it writing a verse
for every mile of Route 77.

When she passes, the security lights
of chain restaurants click off.
The crows do their crow dance
in her tribute. In their language
her name is Popcorn Mother.
The gutters are filled
with winning scratch tickets,
wrinkled from worry and disgrace;
waiting to be understood.
The faces of pawn shops wince
at the sight of her passing.

For you, for once, the sugar-salt-
sorrow-binge won't be as costly.
You locked the keys in the car
but the window is open.
Go into a building with fake palm trees
and stuffed parrots and football helmets on the ceiling,
and eat without guilt.
For you, she is all the small pleasures
in a grinding and nauseous world.

Her hair is like finding the Dollar Store
in a new town. Her hair is like
seeing your dad smile, for a change.
This, is for you. A gift.

Saint Amphetamine

Protect me on this night,
Saint Amphetamine.
The world is a greater darkness than I knew.
I burn my senses on your touch,
and now my intestines are littered
across six hours of midnight highway.
The darkness climbs into the darkness' arms.
Darkness' arms climb into a suit of darkness.
The suit of darkness is hung in a closet of darkness.

Protect me from the moon,
Saint Amphetamine.
It was three-quarters of a silver dollar
over the Missouri River, taut as nickel strings
but now it's a mirror of a forest fire
low to my northwest,
daring to breathe the dawn side
of my medicine face.

At the gas station in Murdo, South Dakota
a one-eyed cat is screaming its head off
at anyone who comes near the door.
At first I thought the bad eye was the moon—
but it's just a full glass of spilled milk,
the milk eye is heavier than
the rest of the head. Its head is twisted
nearly resting on the concrete.
As far as the cat knows
the horizon is a line that divides the self in half
and the stars live next to the earth.

Inside the gas station, everyone is dead.
The clerk is a photograph of a human;
he is either pondering Mount Rushmore,
or the fact that time is a lie.

There is a man in the far corner.
He is wearing an oversized T-shirt
emblazoned with the outline of
Taz the Tasmanian Devil
in red, plastic, jewels.

He is trying on every pair of sunglasses
on the sunglasses rack.
He will never see the light of day again.

IX

magic

Velocity

1.
At three years old
a single year was a third of my life
my life the longest amount
of time I would ever know
the beginning and end of the universe.
At nine years old I realized
that one year was a ninth of my life.
Time was speeding up because
of the life-time I held in my body.
The years grew in inertia
the more I accumulated.
When I was fifteen years old
I discovered I had a body.
One year later I discovered what it could do.
The year after I graduated high school
the world ended. This was the year
I began to find my body again
I had been lost for eight years
for ten years, there was a marriage
and a divorce. And the year
I discovered I had to be responsible for my body.
I kept moving faster
I was chasing the end of body
I was looking for the place
my father lived all the times
I couldn't see him.
I thought my past was just ahead of me.
I thought I could catch up to the beginning of history.
The lovers that tried to know me
discovered there was less and less to know.

I almost became a father
again and again and again.
My best friend, who had taught me
to be a man, who had saved my life
in the backseat of a car, had died.
I crossed the country three times
time zones and calendars slipped away
like sentences of lost poetry.

2.
The first bedroom I ever lived in
that was not my own belonged to my grandfather.
I have changed bedrooms eighteen times since then
but I still live in his body.
Now I work to live Boston
in a family of life-addled gardeners.
We live in an impossibly storied mansion.
A relic from another time.
We are constantly switching rooms—
roommates move in and out and back again.
One generation taking over for another.
The mathematics of the commune
is one of algebra, not arithmetic.
The exponential demands of the pack.
Not just the dishes, but the time.
One day outside the house
is two weeks inside its walls
one year is eight. I have been here over
a decade. A third of my life.

3.
B. Law's mom gave him a computer file
with all the Grateful Dead bootlegs on it.
He made fleets of tapes. Each tape was simply

labeled with the year of the music.
They were being played on every stereo.
While the shower was on, cleaning in the kitchen,
blaring in the piano room.
What year is it? Was the question
tumbling through every door.

Sam Pot is everything
anyone can remember about 1971
alive and crossing the street
trying to make it to another show.
Leonora is burning 1969 at the end
of a cigarette, a black and white
film twisted monochrome psychedelia.
Casey is lifting 1968 on her shoulders
trying to move the cinder block of oppression
with her heart.
Morgan wears 1967 in his beard
knows he found an answer for himself.
Adam has 1867 gathered in the grime
under his fingernails, in the stain
of workingman's madness.
B. Law tells me that no one really understands the Dead
that they're really just a bluegrass band.
That they felt they had no place
in the time they lived
so were reaching for something older.

4.
The question of my inertia kept following me,
I am on the Orange Line home from work.
The train shakes me out of sleep
across the aisle from me is: me
going to work in the morning.

The me from this morning or tomorrow looks at me
leaps across the aisle,
grabs me by the shoulders, shouting,
You're not going anywhere.
Your life is no narrative.
The story builds to no thing.

When I could no longer contain
the velocity inside of me,
I became dozens of people.
For saving my life, I am bound
to tell their story. The years will live together
write music about the movement of bedrooms.
The past is awake long into the morning
laughing and looking to make memories.

The record of our deeds is an ever unfinished house
growing in size as we never reach it.
This is life beyond zenith.
We are the people of every time.

Poem for the Twentieth Century

Your decades stand around like
teenagers loitering on the steps of City Hall.
A villainous zodiac, a shadow tarot.
The children of a deadly music
flirting slowly, waiting
to be carried into the indelible forever.

You are the century that lifted
its skin beyond the sky.
You are the century of devouring.
You did not epoch the empire
of hunger but you made it invisible with its everywhere.

You live so far over the earth
the saints of invention and war
were allowed to explode all over
the sovereign like thin hands.
This pantheon of electric noise
and self-consciousness as currency.
This religion that discovered what
the oceans looked like all at once.

The aughts is a Revenant of Dust
dustier still as it moves toward us
a reminder that coal lead to colonialism.

The teens is a Templar of Silence,
a photograph of mercury, shell shocked.
Knowing the distance violence can take us.
Knowing we needed a war to realize
there was a single planet.

The twenties is an Earthquake of Brass
the long vibrations of breath and bass.
Losing the coins of old kings
her smoke-sex smile hides the hatch
of orphan gods.

The thirties clings to his broken
suspenders even though he knows
he should throw them away.
He has one hand in his pocket.
He might have a gun.

The forties smashed all the ancient symbols
across her sisters' faces.
This blood makeup
becomes arrows we lodge in each others' throats
until everyone joins our choir of mutes.

The fifties wears the nudity of the atom.
Faster than silver, flying into napalm.
Tide burn crackling stone defiance.
The sphere is risen and turning.

When we look into the sixties' eyes
the colors are rainforest vivid.
The delphinium lights the palm,
petals burst from hair mock dynamite.
But something is not right here:
poison in golden crest of collar,
skin that tastes of tank musk.
Her mouth is full of sand.
Her tongue is a series of manacles.

Half a shadow lives on the seventies' shoulder.
His forehead is a tattoo of New York City.
His hands are chained behind his back.
The chain is an American flag.
The flag is on fire.

The eighties is an automobile turned inside out.
We are all its oil.

The nineties' dancehall spine
is shattered under the weight
of her missile-sized cleavage.
Her lips are a fountain of amnesia,
one of her eyes is a mirror.
The other is the Internet.

Century of my creation,
You could not kill the human.
Despite your endless genocide.
Despite the greatest advances in disease
since the plagues.
Despite all the Raptures that have come and gone
and will come again.
We have chosen the earth over heaven every time.

Our history is a lineage of atrocity
but we are still unbroken.
Each generation remains stronger than the last,
despite the war-kings
and the king-merchants, the madness
that slaughters us and pushes us
the death-jazz and the rest of it.

We are the inexhaustible secret.

When every other resource is swallowed
by the last sorcerer,
we will look to each other.
We will look to ourselves
and dig, and dig.

Humanity endures,
and it's time for the twentieth century
to take its place among our relentless maps.
The future has come to replace it.
It is here to do our bidding.

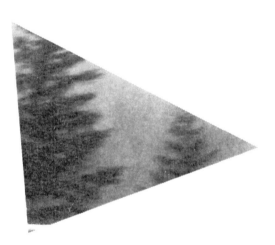

Acknowledgments

Mindy Nettifee, Mike McGee, Jonathan Nathan Sands, Eirean Bradley, Robyn Bateman, Bryan Williams, Kira Clark, Simone Beaubien, Steve Subrizi, Sam Teitel, James Caroline, Karen Finneyfrock, Casey Rocheteau, Adam Ryan Kohl MacCarthy Foam, Morgan Shaker, Kate Lee, Chris North, Sam Franklin, Greg Besun, Brandon Plumert, Greta Merrick, Samuel Potrykus, Shai Erlichman, April Ranger, Leonora Symczak, Stephen Meads, Derrick C. Brown, Eve Connell, and Greg Gerding: Thank You.

About the Author

Brian Stephen Ellis is a transplant to Portland, Oregon from his beloved Boston, Massachusetts. He was a part of the Boston Poetry Slam for six years. He is co-founder of the internationally renowned yes-wave think-tank The Whitehaus Family Record. This is his third book.

UNIVERSITY OF HELL PRESS

CPSIA information can be obtained at www.ICGtesting.com
Printed in the USA
BVOW071639050513

319883BV00001B/4/P